W9-BPN-251

LEAVES

BLACKBIRCH PRESS

An imprint of Thomson Gale, a part of The Thomson Corporation

THOMSON ™

GALE

Detroit • New York • San Francisco • San Diego • New Haven, Conn. • Waterville, Maine • London • Munich

THOMSON

™

GALE

Consultant: Kimi Hosoume
Associate Director of GEMS (Great
Explorations in Math and Science)
Director of PEACHES (Primary
Explorations for Adults, Children,
and Educators in Science)
Lawrence Hall of Science
University of California
Berkeley, California

For The Brown Reference Group plc
Editors: John Farndon and Angela Koo
Picture Researcher: Clare Newman
Design Manager: Lynne Ross
Managing Editor: Bridget Giles
Children's Publisher: Anne O'Daly
Production Director: Alastair Gourlay
Editorial Director: Lindsey Lowe

PHOTOGRAPHIC CREDITS
The Brown Reference Group plc: 16; **Corbis:** W. Perry Conway 15t, Owen Franken 20/21,
Lindsay Hebberd 19, Fritz Polking/FLPA 14; **Ecoscene:** Chinch Gryniewicz 21t; **PhotoDisc:**
PhotoLink 4/5; **Photos.com:** 1, 4t, 9, 10, 11t, 12, 18; **Rex Features:** Marius Alexander 17,
Andrew Drysdale 22.

Front cover: Photos.com

LIBRARY OF CONGRESS CATALOGING-IN-PUBLICATION DATA

Farndon, John.
Leaves / by John Farndon.
p. cm. — (World of plants)
Includes bibliographical references and index.
ISBN 1-4103-0422-1 (lib. : alk. paper)
1. Leaves (Botany)—Juvenile literature. I. Title

QK649.F34 2005
575.5'7—dc22

2005047048

Printed and bound in Thailand
10 9 8 7 6 5 4 3 2 1

Contents

Plant leaves

Nearly all plants have green leaves. The leaves spread out all around the stem to catch the sun.

stem

midrib

veins

▲ Simple leaves

Plain oval leaves like these are called simple leaves. All leaves have lines called veins and midribs.

Some plants have just a few leaves. Tulip flowers, for instance, have just two large leaves shaped like knives. But most plants have many, many more leaves. Trees and bushes often have 50,000 or more. A few really big trees, like giant redwood trees, have several million leaves. Together a plant's leaves are called foliage.

Leaf shapes

Most leaves are thin and flat. The big, flat part of the leaf is called the blade. Tiny pipes or veins criss-cross the blade. The big vein that runs up the middle is called the midrib.

Leaves come in all kinds of shapes and sizes. Some are oval. Some are heart shaped. Some are made from lots of little leaves, or "leaflets," arranged in a pattern. Leaves like these are called compound leaves.

It's Amazing!

The biggest leaves of all belong to the Giant Amazon water lily (below). These leaves can grow up to 8 feet (more than 2 meters) across. They float on the surface of the water. They are so strong that animals and even people can stand on them without sinking.

5

All about leaves

Leaves are a plant's solar panels. They soak up energy from the sun to make food for the plant.

Most leaves are green. That is because they are filled with a green substance. This green substance is called chlorophyll ("KLOR-o-fill"). Chlorophyll helps the plant make food from sunshine.

A plant makes its food from ingredients in air and water from the ground. Air contains a gas called carbon dioxide.

The leaf soaks up carbon dioxide from the air. Water contains a substance called hydrogen. Using the energy of sunlight, the carbon dioxide joins with hydrogen inside the leaf. This makes sugars, the plant's food. Another gas called oxygen is left over. The leaves let out oxygen. All animals need oxygen to breathe.

It's Amazing!

Many plants grow in water. Some water plants catch the sun with long stems that hold their leaves above the water. Others catch it with big leaves that float. But plants like pondweed grow under water. Sun does not shine well through water—especially if the water is dirty. So these plants need lots of leaves.

▶ Making food with sunshine

Here is how a leaf uses sunshine to make sugars from air and water. This process is called photosynthesis ("fo-toe-SIN-thuh-siss").

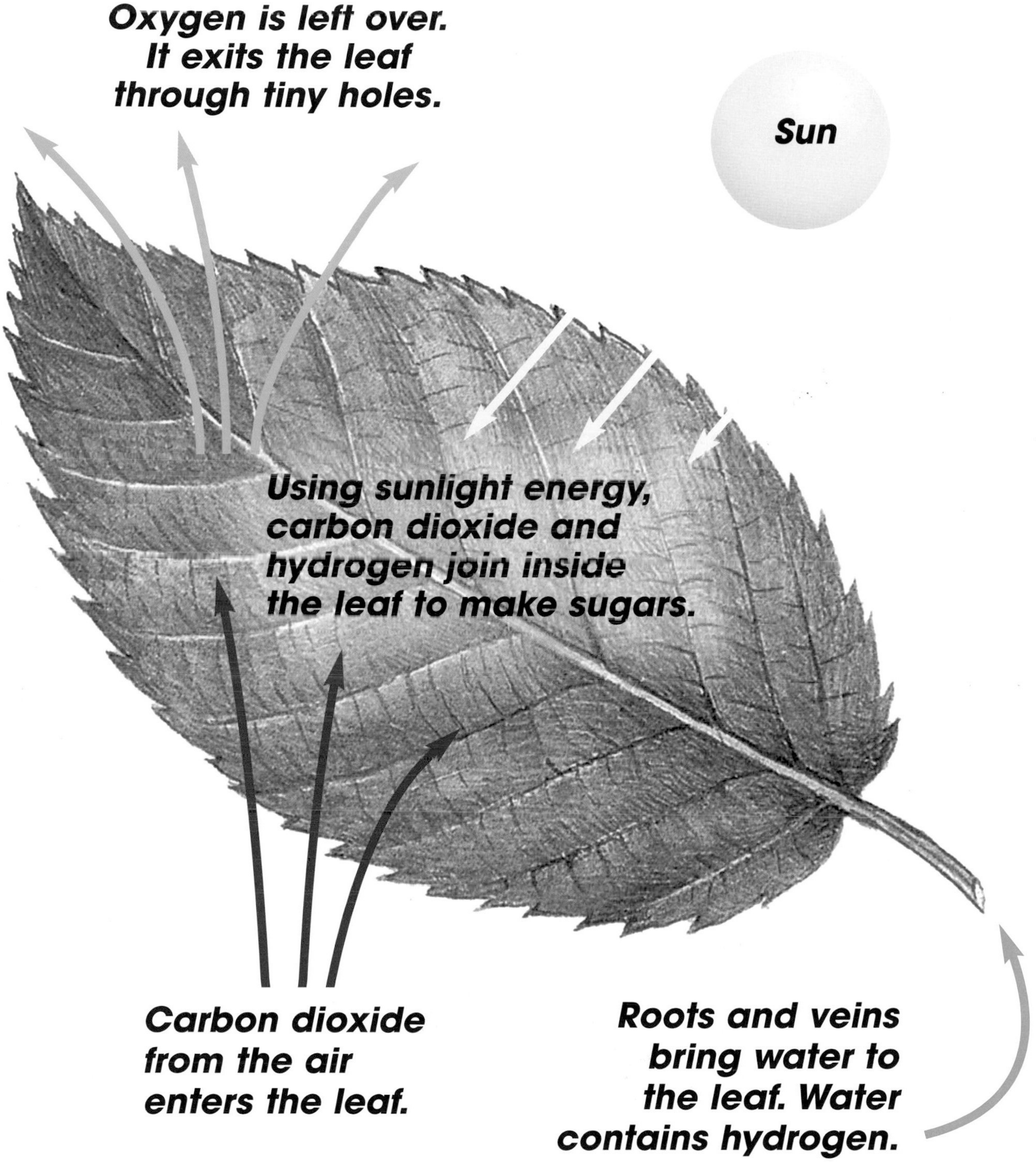

**Oxygen is left over.
It exits the leaf
through tiny holes.**

Sun

7

**Using sunlight energy,
carbon dioxide and
hydrogen join inside
the leaf to make sugars.**

**Carbon dioxide
from the air
enters the leaf.**

**Roots and veins
bring water to
the leaf. Water
contains hydrogen.**

How leaves change

All leaves start life on a plant as tiny packets called buds. Buds have a tough covering called scales. Scales stop the bud from getting cold in winter. The baby leaf is curled up snugly inside the scales.

In spring, the scales open up and the baby leaf pops out, still curled up. But the leaf quickly uncurls and flattens out in the warm sunshine. Soon it grows into a full-size leaf, ready for the summer sun.

Fall colors

In summer there is lots of sun and water for leaves to make food. In winter, the sun shines less and water is often frozen. So in fall some tree leaves stop making food. They lose the chlorophyll they use to make food. Chlorophyll makes leaves green. When leaves lose chlorophyll, they lose their green and hidden orange and yellow colors show through. That is why trees turn red and gold in fall.

Try This!

Make your own pictures of fall leaves. Choose some leaves and lay them in a nice pattern on white paper. Place another sheet of white paper on top. With a wax crayon gently rub over the paper and see the leaves magically appear.

▶ Fallen leaves

When a tree's leaves change color in fall, the stalk of each leaf withers. The stalk becomes so weak that the leaf drops off the tree. Before long, the ground beneath the tree is covered in fallen leaves.

Evergreen leaves

Not all trees lose their leaves in fall. Some keep their leaves all year round, even in midwinter. Trees like that are are called evergreens. Many trees that grow in very cold places are evergreen. The forests of northern Canada are mostly evergreen. So, too, are many forests on mountains.

By staying green all through winter, evergreens can still use the winter sunshine to make food. Being able to make food in winter helps them since their summers are short and cool.

Coping with cold

Evergreen leaves that grow in cool places have to be very tough to survive freezing winter weather. To help them stay warm, evergreen leaves often have a thick, waxy coat. The leaves are often thin like needles, too, so there is very little leaf to get cold.

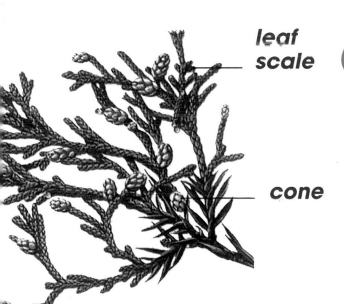

leaf scale

cone

◀▲ Needles and scales

Pine trees have evergreen leaves like needles (left). Cypresses have evergreen leaves with tiny scales (above).

It's Amazing!

Most pine needles are less than 4 inches (10 centimeters) long. That is shorter than this panel of text. North America's coulter pine (above) has needles more than 1 foot (half a meter) long. It also has seed cones so large they could kill a person if one dropped on his or her head. That is why the coulter pine is also called the widowmaker.

11

Leaves and animals

All kinds of animals have special relationships with leaves. For many animals leaves make tasty food.

▲ Browsers
Giraffes live in Africa. Their long necks help them eat leaves that are hard to reach. These leaves are often the juiciest.

Leaves are full of nutrients. That is why animals from giant elephants to tiny insects eat leaves. Animals that eat leaves from trees and bushes are called browsers. Antelopes and deer are browsers. So are giraffes and elephants. Animals that eat leaves from the ground are grazers. Sheep and cows are grazers. They eat grass leaves.

Insects and leaves

Many insects feed on leaves when they are young. Some female insects lay their eggs on leaves. When the eggs hatch, the young insects have a meal ready and waiting for them. Caterpillars are young butterflies and moths. Caterpillars need to grow big quickly. So they munch their way through lots of leaves.

▶ Leaf-cutter ants

Leaf-cutter ants snip off pieces of a leaf with their sharp pincers. The ants line up and carry the leaves back to their nest. Often the leaf is much bigger than the ant!

It's Amazing!

Leaf-cutter ants cut leaves from trees to take to their underground nest. The ants do not eat the leaves. Instead they chew them up and spit them out to make a kind of soil. The ants grow a kind of fungus using this soil. The ants eat the fungus. They also feed it to their young.

13

Meat eaters

▲ Sundew

The sundew's leaves are edged with hairs. At the tip of each hair is a sticky, syrupy droplet.

Some plants cannot survive only on the sugars made by their leaves. They need extra food—meat! The sundew plant grows in poor soil, so it needs to trap insects as food. When a juicy insect comes near, it becomes tangled in the leaf's sticky hairs.

The leaf folds over the fly and traps it. Special plant juices turn the insect into a thick, soupy liquid food.

Disappearing trick

The pitcher plant is another insect catcher. Its leaves are shaped like jugs (pitchers), and they have slippery sides. So if an insect accidentally falls in, it gets caught.

Try This!

The Venus flytrap (above) has a hinged leaf that snaps shut on insect victims. If you grow your own flytrap plant at home, you can feed it small bugs such as fruit flies or gnats. Then watch the plant snap them up! You can buy Venus flytraps at garden stores and plant nurseries.

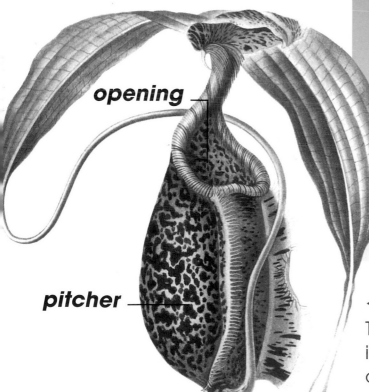

opening

pitcher

◄ Pitcher plant

The largest pitcher plants, in Borneo, have pitchers that can catch rats, frogs, or lizards!

15

How leaves survive

Many animals eat leaves. So leaves have to defend themselves. Some plants have leaves that are very tough to chew. Other leaves have very sharp edges. Holly leaves have spikes that stop animals from eating them. Mimosa leaves fold up out of harm's way when they are touched.

Some leaves fight with chemicals. Some simply taste bad. Some sting to the touch. Some are poisonous to animals that eat them. Mustard, cabbage, and radish leaves contain chemicals that taste nice and sharp to people. But the same chemicals are strong enough to kill many small insects that try to feed on the leaves.

▶ **Thistles**

Thistles have sharp tough leaves. This puts off most animals. Animals such as goats have very tough mouths, though. They happily eat thistles, spikes and all.

It's Amazing!

In a few weeks, these caterpillars will turn into giant lunar moths. First they must grow fast by eating a lot of leaves. If a human baby grew as fast it would soon be as big as an elephant. But all caterpillars are big leaf eaters. This is why some leaves defend themselves with chemicals.

lunar moth caterpillar

Leaves and people

Eating leaves helps people stay healthy. Leaves are also used to make paper, homes to live in, and much more.

▲ Cabbage leaves

Cabbage leaves are nourishing food. They contain a chemical called vitamin C, which helps people stay healthy.

People get ill if they do not get certain vital chemicals in their food. These chemicals are called vitamins and minerals. Leaves are packed with them. Unfortunately, you cannot eat just any leaf. Most leaves are too tough to eat. Some even make you sick.

But many vegetables have big, soft, green leaves that are very good to eat. These vegetables are called green vegetables. The best-known green vegetables are cabbage, spinach, chard, kale, lettuce, and sprouts.

Tasty leaves

Leaves can help make food tastier, too. Many leaves are added to food to make better flavors. These flavoring leaves come from small plants called herbs. They include rosemary, thyme, sage, mint, oregano, and parsley.

▶ Tea leaves

Tea leaves are picked by hand when they are young and green. They are dried and sometimes toasted. That is why tea leaves in packets are brown.

It's Amazing!

Tea is the most popular drink in the world after water. A billion cups of tea are drunk around the world every day! Tea is made from leaves of the tea bush. Most of the tea we drink comes from warm places such as India, China, and Sri Lanka in Asia, and Kenya in Africa. Tea grows best high up on hills in these warm countries.

19

How people use leaves

People use leaves for many things besides food. Big leaves like banana leaves can be used to build shelters. Banana leaves grow up to 6 feet (2 meters) long. They are tough enough to make good roofs! Palm leaves make good roofs, too. Raffia palm leaves can also be torn up to make fibers. The fibers are then woven together to make clothes and rugs.

Some leaves like citronella make a nice-smelling oil. Such oils are put into perfumes and soaps. Mint and wintergreen leaves have oils that taste good. These are added to foods.

Leaves can even make colors. Leaves like indigo and henna are dried and ground into powder. The powders give colorings called dyes. Indigo gives purple dye. Henna gives a red dye.

▼ Banana umbrella

Banana leaves are very useful. In the warm places where they grow, people use banana leaves as instant umbrellas. The leaves are used to make shopping bags, too. And they are also used instead of plastic to wrap food and can even be used as plates for food.

It's Amazing!

Long ago, ancient Egyptians made paper called papyrus. Papyrus comes from a tall, grasslike plant called a reed. This reed grows along the Nile River in Egypt. Papyrus is made from the dried and flattened leaves of the reed. When the Egyptians wrote on papyrus, instead of using letters they drew pictures. These pictures are called hieroglyphs ("HI-ro-glifs").

21

Magic leaves

In olden times, people believed leaves that stay green through winter like holly and laurel were special. Holly leaves are still a favorite decoration in places where people celebrate Christmas. Long ago, in ancient Greece, people carried laurel leaves for good luck.

The first Olympic Games were held in Greece at least 3,500 years ago. When Greek athletes won races, they were given wreaths (rings) of laurel leaves to wear on their head. This still happens at the Olympics today. Roman generals also wore laurel wreaths after great war victories.

◄ Holly leaves
Many people in some Christian countries put holly up at Christmas. Holly reminds people of the crown of thorns worn by Jesus. The red berries represent droplets of blood.

Glossary

blade the flat surface of a leaf.

browser a leaf-eating animal.

bud a curled up new leaf.

chlorophyll a green substance in leaves. It helps the leaf use sunlight to make sugary food.

evergreen a plant that keeps its leaves green all the year round.

foliage all the leaves on a plant.

grazer a grass-eating animal.

hydrogen a gas that helps make up water.

midrib the stiff rod down the center of a leaf.

oxygen a gas in the air. Together with hydrogen it makes up water.

photosynthesis the way leaves use energy from sunlight to make sugary food.

scales the covers on a bud.

sugars energy food.

veins the tiny pipes in leaves that carry water and other substances.

vitamins substances people and animals need in tiny amounts to stay healthy.

Find out more

Books

Susan Blackaby, Charlene Delage. *A Book About Leaves (Growing Things).* Minneapolis: Picture Window Books, 2003.
Melanie S. Mitchell. *Leaves.* Minneapolis: Lerner Books, 2004.

Web site

USGS Kids Corner
biology.usgs.gov/features/ kidscorner/kcprojct.html

Index

24